BOOK OF **AFFIRMATIONS** FOR **CHILDREN**

ASHLEY WHITLATCH

Illustrations by Carly Christensen

A.K. Publishing
Peoria, IL

I AM EVERYTHING: BOOK OF AFFIRMATIONS FOR CHILDREN
A.K. Publishing
Peoria, IL

I AM EVERYTHING: BOOK OF AFFIRMATIONS FOR CHILDREN © 2020 Ashley Whitlatch

All rights reserved. This book or parts thereof may not be reproduced in any form, stored in a retrieval system, or transmitted in any form by any means – electronic, mechanical, photocopy, recording, or otherwise – without prior written permission of the publisher, except as provided by the United States of America copyright law.

Hardcover ISBN: 978-0-578-77300-1

Printed in the United States of America
First Edition: November 2020

Cover Design: Make Your Mark Publishing Solutions
Interior Layout: Make Your Mark Publishing Solutions
Illustrations: Carly Christensen

DEDICATION

For my children, Alianna and Kyrin, and my niece, A'Nyijah.
May you be the best version of you in this world.

In Loving Memory of Hayven M. Porter.

I am **everything**.

**Anything is possible,
as long as I believe in myself.**

Believing in myself means I know I can do *anything* I put my *mind* to, even if it's something I don't think I can do.

I will do everything with all my might.
I know I will make mistakes, which is okay,
as long as I learn what's wrong from right.

I know I can **overcome** and **beat anything** that may seem hard to do, even something that may make me feel **blue**.

I know I may not feel confident at times, but I won't forget that I am one of a kind.

I have a beautiful heart and
I know I am smart.

I know my smile can make others smile, too, because it's all about the little things we do.

I am amazing, and I am stronger than anything negative I may be facing.

I can be inspiring, and even if I feel sad or mad, I will be sure to always keep climbing.

Just like a light, I will shine. No one can put it out, not even the feeling of doubt.

I am great and I will not let my heart be filled with hate.

I am me. I know what I can be.

I am everything.

ACKNOWLEDGEMENTS

Firstly, I would like to thank God because with Him, all things are possible. I would like to acknowledge my mother, Penny, for being the best mother, friend, and support system that a girl could ever need. I would also like to thank all of my loved ones who have been a part of my journey of growth and a constant reminder of encouragement.